On the List

Written by Jo Windsor
Illustrated by Richard Hoit

Jon and Mary's Wedding Cake

For the Cake Mix
24 eggs
flour
1 packet juice

Cake Icing
6 lemons
icing sugar

For the Decorations

fish

River Ride Trip:

Things I Need To Be Safe
Helmet
Goggles
Torch
Wetsuit
Flippers
Life jacket
Other Things
Canoe
Paddles
Clothes (in wet bag)
Food
Towels

Butterfly Hunting Trip:

Things to Take
Boxes – big and small,
with holes
Butterfly nets
Magnifying glass
Butterfly book
Notebook
Pencil
Map
Tent
Sleeping bag
Food

Things to Take

Big purple pants
White gloves
Spotty tie
Top hat
Red nose
Big flat shoes
Rabbits
e with one wheel
orn
Bucket

2

Picnic Basket

cheese
bread
butter
tomatoes
drink
fruit
cake

Other Gear

rugs
pillows
~~ons~~
s
~~t~~

net
ball and
sunglas
books
sunscr
towel

Building Materials:

Wood
Nails
Trap doors
Springs

Mouse Food:

Peanut butter
Cheese
Small pieces of apple
Seeds

Birthday Party List

Meats

12 hens
6 turkeys

Other Food

12 boxes of eggs
10 baskets fruit
3 sacks of potatoes
8 cabbages

Party Things

54 cake candles
60 party hats
60 balloons

Lists

Hello, I'm Wally.
I make the biggest and best cakes in town. I make birthday cakes, party cakes, and wedding cakes. The next cake I have to make is a big wedding cake for Jon and Mary Smith. They are having 300 people at their wedding. When I have a big cake to do, I make a list.

Jon and Mary's Wedding Cake

For the Cake Mix
24 eggs
flour
1 packet juice

Cake Icing
6 lemons
icing sugar

For the Decorations
jelly beans
chocolate fish
silver balls
nuts
ribbon

FLOUR

Hello, I'm Sue.
I'm a River Rider. I love riding the rivers. The rivers I ride can be dangerous. When you ride rivers, you need special gear. Here is a list of the things I take:

River Ride Trip:

Things I Need To Be Safe
Helmet
Goggles
Torch
Wetsuit
Flippers
Life jacket
Other Things
Canoe
Paddles
Clothes (in wet bag)
Food
Towels

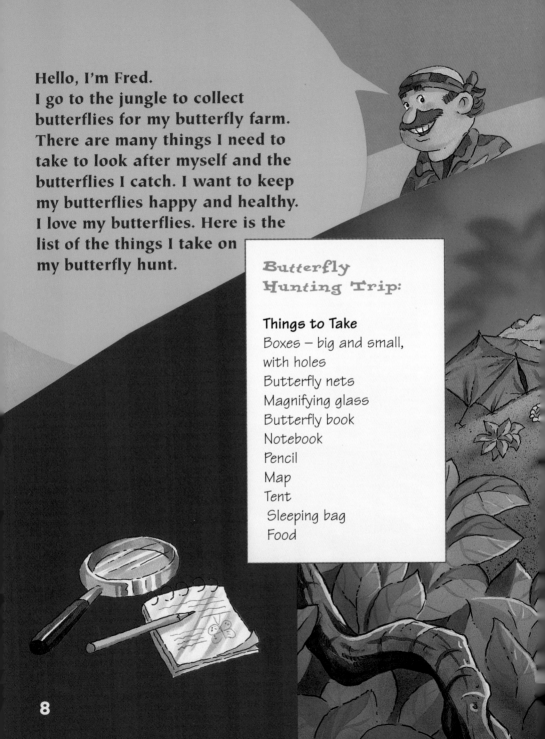

Hello, I'm Fred.
I go to the jungle to collect butterflies for my butterfly farm. There are many things I need to take to look after myself and the butterflies I catch. I want to keep my butterflies happy and healthy. I love my butterflies. Here is the list of the things I take on my butterfly hunt.

Butterfly Hunting Trip:

Things to Take
Boxes — big and small, with holes
Butterfly nets
Magnifying glass
Butterfly book
Notebook
Pencil
Map
Tent
Sleeping bag
Food

Hello, I'm Cook.
The king is having a
birthday party. It is a very
busy time for me. I have to
get up early and visit the
market to get things for the
birthday party. Here is my
shopping list.

Birthday Party List

Meats
12 hens
6 turkeys

Other Food
12 boxes of eggs
10 baskets fruit
3 sacks of potatoes
8 cabbages

Party Things
54 cake candles
60 party hats
60 balloons

Hello, I'm Clown.
I go to lots of birthday parties.
I make the kids laugh. I have
to make sure I take all the
things I need for my tricks.
I make a list so that I don't
forget anything!

Things to Take:

Big purple pants
White gloves
Spotty tie
Top hat
Red nose
Big flat shoes
Rabbits
Bike with one wheel
Horn
Bucket

Hello, I'm Mr Green.
I have a big family that loves
to go to the lake. The kids like
to swim, fish, and play ball. Mrs
Green likes to read and I like to
sleep. Before we go, I write a list
of all the things we need to take.

Picnic Basket

cheese
bread
butter
tomatoes
drink
fruit
cake

Other Gear

rugs	net
pillows	ball and bat
cushions	sunglasses
games	books
hats	sunscreen
fly swat	towels

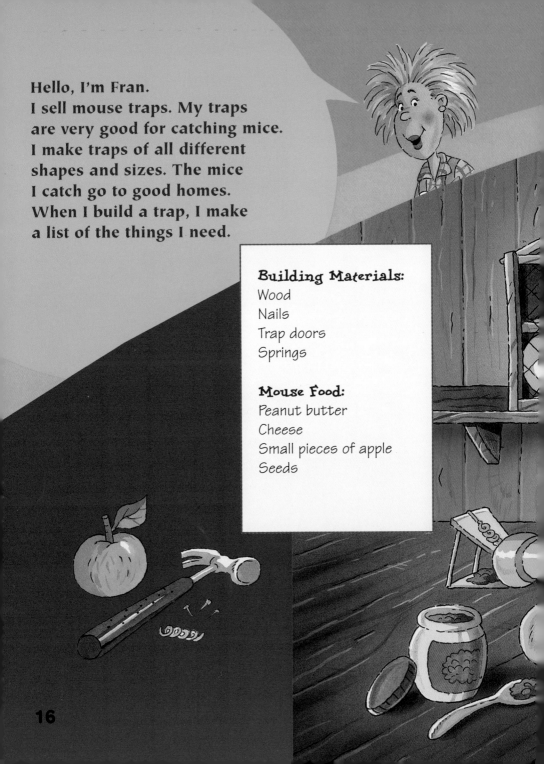

Hello, I'm Fran.
I sell mouse traps. My traps
are very good for catching mice.
I make traps of all different
shapes and sizes. The mice
I catch go to good homes.
When I build a trap, I make
a list of the things I need.

Building Materials:
Wood
Nails
Trap doors
Springs

Mouse Food:
Peanut butter
Cheese
Small pieces of apple
Seeds

16

Lists

You can write lists for:

What to take
Where to go
What to wear
What to buy
What you need
What to do

How to write a list

Step One
Think about:

- Why am I writing this list
- What is the list for
- What things do I want on my list

Step Two
Write down the things you want on your list.

(You could write headings for your list to sort the things into groups.)

Step Three
Check your list:

- Have you forgotten anything?
- Is there anything you can take off your list?

Remember
You can use your list as a checklist. You can tick off the things you have got or have done.

Shopping List for Mum's Party:

Food
Cake
Strawberries
Cherries
Chocolate

Decorations for Cake
Candles
Silver Beads
Ribbons

Fun things
Party Hats
Balloons

Guide Notes

Title: On the List
Stage: Fluency (1)

Text Form: Lists
Approach: Guided Reading
Processes: Thinking Critically, Exploring Language, Processing Information
Written and Visual Focus: List, Speech Bubbles

THINKING CRITICALLY
(sample questions)
- Where would Wally go to get the things that he has written on his list?
- Why do you think Fran included food on her list?
- Why do you think Fred included a map on his list?
- What do you think would happen if Cook forgot to put the candles on her list. What would the king say?

EXPLORING LANGUAGE

Terminology
Spread, author and illustrator credits, ISBN number

Vocabulary
Clarify: silver, collect, magnifying glass, market, cushions, springs, fly swat, gear
Nouns: cake, river, map, list
Verbs: ride, hunt, fish
Singular/plural: mouse/mice, butterfly/butterflies, egg/eggs, canoe/canoes

Print Conventions
Colon, dash (boxes – big and small), apostrophes – possessive (Mary's wedding cake), contraction (I'm, don't), brackets: (in wet bag)

Phonological Patterns
Focus on short and long vowel **i** (list, fish, trip, time, tie, mice)
Discuss base words – biggest, parties, dangerous, butterflies
Look at suffix **ous** (danger**ous**)